Psychologists and Their Theories for Students

Product Manager
Meggin Condino **Project Editor**
Kristine Krapp **Editorial**
Mark Springer

Indexing Services
Katherine Jensen **Rights and Aquisitions**
Margaret Abendroth, Ann Taylor **Imaging and Multimedia**
Robyn Young, Lezlie Light, Dan Newell **Product Design**
Pamela A. Galbreath **Manufacturing**
Evi Seoud, Lori Kessler © 2005, 2015 Gale, a part of Cengage Learning Inc.

For more information, contact
Gale, an imprint of Cengage Learning
27500 Drake Rd.
Farmington Hills, MI 48331-3535

LIBRARY OF CONGRESS CATALOGING-IN-PUBLICATION DATA

Psychologists and their theories for students / Kristine Krapp, editor.

    p. cm.

        Includes bibliographical references and index.
        ISBN 0-7876-6543-6 (set : hardcover : alk. paper) —
        ISBN 0-7876-6544-4 (v. 1) —
        ISBN 0-7876-6545-2 (v. 2)
        1. Psychologists. 2. Psychology.
        I. Krapp, Kristine M.

BF109.A1P72 2004

150'.92'2—dc22   2004011589

Printed in the United States of America 10 9 8 7 6 5
4 3 2 1

Albert Bandura

1925-

**CANADIAN-BORN   AMERICAN
PSYCHOLOGIST, RESEARCHER**

UNIVERSITY OF IOWA, PhD, 1952

BRIEF OVERVIEW

When people first try a new sport, they often know what they need to do before ever stepping onto a playing field or court because they've watched other people play. Albert Bandura recognized the importance of this process, called observational learning or vicarious learning, in which people learn to do something without actually performing the behavior themselves or being directly rewarded or punished for it. The advantage of this kind of learning is that it lets people learn from the experience of others, without having to reinvent the wheel every time they do something new.

In a series of classic studies, Bandura and his colleagues looked at the way observational learning affects aggressive behavior in children. Some children were shown a film in which an adult punched, hammered, and kicked a plastic inflatable doll, called a Bobo doll. Those who viewed the film were later more likely to act aggressively themselves when given a chance to play with the doll. Furthermore, seeing the adult in the film be rewarded for aggression increased the likelihood of aggression in the children even more, while seeing the adult punished had the opposite effect. However, just watching the aggressive behavior was enough for the children to learn it, regardless of whether rewards or punishments were given. The Bobo doll experiments became some of the best-known studies in psychology.

Yet, as important as observational learning is, Bandura also stressed that people have self-control over which behaviors they copy and which they do not. This self-control is exercised through cognitive, or thought, processes. Bandura's other major contribution to psychology has been the description of one key cognitive process, called perceived self-efficacy. People's perceived self-efficacy refers to their beliefs about how capably they will be able to perform a behavior in a particular situation.

These two central themes in Bandura's work—observational learning and self-efficacy beliefs—have been brought together with other factors under the label "social-cognitive theory." According to Bandura's social-cognitive theory, the outer world and the inner person—including that person's beliefs, thoughts, and feelings—combine to determine an individual's actions. The results of those actions, in turn, help shape the person's future beliefs, thoughts, and feelings. In this way, a cycle is established, in which the outer world, the inner person, and the person's behavior all act on and feed off each other. However, this does not necessarily have to be a vicious cycle. In fact, by changing his or her self-efficacy beliefs, a person can potentially break free of an old, negative cycle and establish a new, positive one. This theory is the culmination of Bandura's lifetime of study and research.

In 2002, a psychologist named Steven Haggbloom and his colleagues published a paper in which they attempted to rank the 100 most eminent psychologists of the twentieth century. They based their ranking on six different variables: citations in journals, mentions in introductory psychology textbooks, a survey of American Psychological Society members, election as president of the American Psychological Association (APA) or receipt of the APA Distinguished Scientific Contributions Award, membership in the National

Academy of Sciences, and use of the psychologist's surname to identify a particular theory or school of psychology. Bandura ranked number four, right behind B.F. Skinner, Jean Piaget, and Sigmund Freud.

BIOGRAPHY

Growing up in a remote village in Canada, Bandura attended a small school where teachers and textbooks were in short supply. Perhaps because of these limitations, Bandura became a self-motivated and independent learner. His curiosity and independence would serve him well throughout a long and productive career.

Childhood in Canada

Bandura was born on December 4, 1925, the youngest child and the only boy of six children. His parents were both immigrants who had come to Canada from Eastern Europe as adolescents. His mother was originally from the Ukraine, and his father, from Poland. Neither had a formal education, but they valued learning highly. For example, Bandura's father taught himself to read three languages: Polish, Russian, and German.

Bandura grew up in Mundare, a tiny community in northern Alberta, Canada, about 50 miles (80 km) east of Edmonton. There, he attended the only school in town. The little school was woefully short on both teachers and supplies. Two teachers taught all the high school classes, and the high school math class had only a single textbook for everyone, including the teacher, to share. As a result, the students were left largely to their own devices. One might expect that this situation would produce students who were illprepared for the larger world. Instead, it seems to have pushed the students to take charge of their own educations, and many of them went on to attend universities around the globe. As Bandura was later quoted on an Emory University Web site in his honor, "The content of most textbooks is perishable, but the tools of self-directedness serve one well over time."

The college years

When it came time for college, Bandura headed for the University of British Columbia in Vancouver. Once there, he stumbled onto psychology by chance. Bandura was carpooling to school with a group of other students who were early risers. He signed up for an introductory psychology class just to fill the early morning time slot, but he quickly became fascinated with the subject. Within three years, in 1949, he had graduated with a prize in psychology. Years later, Bandura discussed how personal actions often place people in situations where fortunate events can then shape the future course of their lives.

For graduate school, Bandura settled on the University of Iowa. At the time, the psychology department there was a hotbed of research and scholarly activity. Among the distinguished faculty members were Kenneth Spence and Kurt Lewin. Spence was known for his research on learning and conditioning. Earlier, Spence had studied with Clark Hull, a leading figure in behaviorism, a school of psychology that posits that organisms can be trained, or conditioned, to respond in specific ways to specific stimuli. At Iowa, Spence extended Hull's theories and research in an effort to come up with a precise mathematical formula to describe the learning of behavior. The two men's research on learning became known collectively as the Hull-Spence theory.

Lewin, on the other hand, had a rather different approach to the study of human behavior—an approach he called field theory. Lewin held that a person's behavior arises from complex interactions among psychological factors inside the person, environmental factors outside the person, and the relationship between these inner and outer worlds. Lewin proposed his field theory as a method for analyzing these kinds of causal relationships.

It must have been a very exciting time and place for Bandura. As he later recalled in a book by Richard Evans:

> I found Iowa to be intellectually lively, but also very supportive. . .At Iowa we were imprinted early on a model of scholarship that combined high respect for theory linked to venturesome research. It was an excellent beginning for a career.

Bandura also found time for nonacademic interests. One day, while golfing with a friend, he found himself playing behind a pair of female golfers. Eventually, he wound up in a sand trap with one of the women, Virginia Varns, who was on the teaching staff at the College of Nursing. The two struck up an acquaintance that blossomed into a lifelong romance. Bandura and Varns were married in 1952, the same year Bandura finished his PhD in clinical psychology. The couple went on to have two daughters: Mary, born in 1954, and Carol, born in 1958.

Career at Stanford

In 1953, Bandura took a job as an instructor in the psychology department at Stanford University. He has remained at Stanford ever since, becoming a full professor in 1964. In 1974, Stanford awarded Bandura an endowed chair, a high honor in the academic world, and he became the David Starr Jordan Professor of Social Science in Psychology. The intellectual climate at Stanford has served Bandura well, providing eminent colleagues and bright students with whom to conduct research and exchange ideas.

Perhaps the first prominent colleague to influence Bandura at Stanford was Robert Sears, who was chairman of the psychology department when Bandura arrived. Among other things, Sears was studying child-rearing patterns that led to aggressiveness and dependency in children. Following this line of work, Bandura and his first graduate student, Richard Walters, began studying the family backgrounds of very aggressive delinquents. They discovered that one factor affecting aggression among teenagers was whether or not the teens' parents were hostile or aggressive. In 1959, Bandura and Walters published a book titled *Adolescent Aggression,* which described their research on this subject.

Bandura was struck by the seeming influence of parental role models on teenagers' aggressive behavior. He wanted to study this effect in more depth experimentally, but first he had to come up with a workable study design. The result was the now-famous Bobo doll experiments, which Bandura conducted with Dorothea Ross and Sheila Ross. In 1963, the findings from this research were summarized in a second book with Walters, titled *Social Learning and Personality Development.* Few areas of psychological research have ever captured the public imagination as well as the Bobo doll studies did. As Bandura told Evans, "When I'm introduced at invited lectures at other universities, the students place a Bobo doll by the lectern. From time to time I have been asked to autograph one. The Bobo doll has achieved stardom in psychological circles."

Of course, it was Bandura himself who was really the rising star. In 1964, in addition to being made a professor at Stanford, he was elected a Fellow of the APA. During the 1969–70 school year, he was awarded a fellowship at the Center for Advanced Study in the Behavioral Sciences, a center near Stanford that brings together scientists and scholars from around the world who show exceptional accomplishment or promise in their fields. In 1969, Bandura published *Principles of Behavior Modification,* the first important book in cognitive behavior therapy. In 1974, Bandura received his endowed chair at Stanford, and, during the 1976–77 school year, he served as chairman of the psychology department there.

PRINCIPAL PUBLICATIONS

- With R. H. Walters. *Adolescent Aggression.* New York: Ronald Press, 1959.

- With R. H. Walters. *Social Learning and Personality Development.* New York: Holt, Rinehart & Winston, 1963.

- *Principles of Behavior Modification.* New York: Holt, Rinehart & Winston, 1969.

- Editor. *Psychological Modeling: Conflicting Theories.* Chicago: Aldine-Atherton Press, 1971.

- *Aggression: A Social Learning Analysis.* Englewood Cliffs, NJ: Prentice-Hall, 1973.

- "Self-Efficacy: Toward a Unifying Theory of Behavioral Change." *Psychological Review* 84 (1977) 191–215.

- *Social Learning Theory.* Englewood Cliffs, NJ: Prentice-Hall, 1977.

- *Social Foundations of Thought and Action: A Social Cognitive Theory.* Englewood Cliffs, NJ: Prentice-Hall, 1986.

- Editor. *Self-Efficacy in Changing Societies.* New York: Cambridge University Press, 1995.

- *Self-Efficacy: The Exercise of Control.* New York: Freeman, 1997.

Meanwhile, Bandura continued his ambitious research program. In 1977, he offered a theoretical framework for his findings in *Social Learning Theory*. This book had a dramatic impact on psychology. It heralded a great upsurge in interest in social learning theory among other psychologists during the 1980s.

By this time, however, it was already growing apparent to Bandura that something was missing from his theory. In a 1977 paper, titled "Self-Efficacy: Toward a Unifying Theory of Behavioral Change," he identified the missing piece as self-beliefs. Soon, Bandura had broadened his social learning theory to include a wide range of self-beliefs and self-control abilities. He described a system in which a person's beliefs, thoughts, feelings, and physical responses interact with both the environment and the person's behavior. He then renamed his expanded theory the "social-cognitive theory," both to distinguish it from other social learning theories of the day and to stress the central importance of beliefs and thoughts. In 1986, Bandura published *Social Foundations of Thought and Action: A Social Cognitive Theory,* which set forth his new theory of human functioning.

The linchpin of social-cognitive theory is self-efficacy. In the last few decades, Bandura has continued to explore this concept and its many practical applications. Researchers around the world have taken up the torch as well. In 1993, a scientific conference was held in Germany on young people's beliefs about their personal efficacy to meet the demands of a rapidly changing world. Bandura later edited a book, titled *Self-Efficacy in Changing Societies,* containing papers presented at the conference. Then, in 1997, he published *Self-Efficacy: The Exercise of Control,* in which he set forth his detailed ideas about the causes and effects of self-efficacy beliefs.

Lifetime of achievement

Over the years, Bandura has collected numerous awards and honors. These include a Guggenheim Fellowship (1972), the APA Distinguished Scientific Contributions Award (1980), the APA William James Award (1989), the APA Thorndike Award for Distinguished Contributions of Psychology to Education (1999), and the Lifetime Achievement Award from the Association for the Advancement of Behavior Therapy (2001). He is a member of the Institute of Medicine of the National Academy of Sciences. He has also received 14 honorary degrees from universities around the world.

In return, Bandura has given generously of his time and energy to the field of psychology. He has held a number of offices in scientific societies, including serving as APA president in 1974 and being named honorary president of the Canadian Psychological Association in 1999. He has also sat on the editorial boards of some 30 journals. In addition, he has authored seven books and edited two others. Several of his books have been translated into languages such as Polish, Spanish, Portuguese, German, Japanese, Russian, French, Italian, and Korean. Today, Bandura's name and ideas are familiar to psychologists and psychology students worldwide.

In his late seventies, at a age when most people have long since retired, Bandura continues to publish and make contributions to psychology. His most recent interests include the psychological impact of electronic media, the means by which people affect their own motivation and behavior, the way people view their self-efficacy to influence events in their lives, and the source of stress reactions and depression.

THEORIES

Perhaps the most notable aspect of Bandura's long career is the number of significant contributions he has made through the decades. In the 1960s, he published classic research on observational learning and modeling. In the 1970s, he expanded upon these findings to develop an influential theory of social learning. In the 1980s, this evolved into a social-cognitive theory of human functioning. And in the 1990s, Bandura further refined his ideas about self-efficacy. In recent years, his followers have found widespread practical uses for self-efficacy theory in education, mental health, physical health, sports, business, and politics.

Observational learning and modeling

Main points Behaviorism, the dominant school of psychology when Bandura was a student, holds that people are conditioned, or trained, to respond in certain ways by rewards and punishments. Bandura soon realized that this could not be the whole explanation for how people learn. It would take several lifetimes to learn all the complicated responses that people need to know by rewards and punishments alone. Bandura suggested that there must be a way that people can learn simply by watching others, thereby removing the need to learn everything by tedious trial-and-error.

This process of learning by watching others is called observational learning or vicarious learning. It is closely related to the concept of modeling, in which people fashion themselves after the image of another. According to Bandura, people do not just mindlessly mimic whatever they see. Instead, although people may learn a multitude of behaviors by observation, they consciously decide which ones to actually copy.

Explanation One powerful factor influencing whether or not a behavior will be copied is the expected outcome. Bandura's research showed that people are more likely to copy behavior that they expect will lead to a positive outcome. However, this expectation is not rooted only in the actual rewards and punishments that people have seen. It is also based on anticipated consequences; in other words, on people's beliefs about what will happen.

Several other factors may also affect the likelihood that an observed behavior will be imitated:

- Characteristics of the person being observed—For example, studies have found that the person's age, sex, similarity to the observer, status, skill, and power may all be important.

- Characteristics of the observer—For example, research has shown that people with low self-esteem, those who are more dependent, and those who have been rewarded in the past for imitative behavior are more likely to copy someone else. In addition, the observer obviously must have the necessary mental and physical skills to carry out the task.

- Characteristics of the behavior—For example, behavior that is simple or admired is more likely to be imitated.

Examples In the famous Bobo doll experiments, Bandura and his colleagues showed some children a film in which an adult hit, hammered, and kicked the inflatable doll. These children were more likely than ones who had not seen the film to later hit and kick the doll themselves when given a chance to play with it. This tendency was strengthened if the adult in the film was rewarded for aggressive behavior, and the tendency was weakened if the adult was punished. However, just seeing the aggressive behavior was enough for the children to learn it, even when no rewards or punishments were given.

Of course, Bandura was not the first person to note that people often learn by copying others. Anyone who has spent time around young children, for instance, has undoubtedly noticed how they mimic their parents. Two decades before the Bobo doll experiments, Neal Miller and John Dollard had published the first scholarly book about observational learning, titled *Social Learning and Imitation*. Miller and Dollard's work was still in the behaviorist mode, but they construed conditioning more broadly than had earlier theorists. They emphasized not only personal and social rewards, but also factors such as motivations and drives. Bandura took these ideas a step further. More than any other psychologist, Bandura built a solid foundation of scientific evidence about how observational learning actually occurs, with or without rewards and punishments. In so doing, he helped the study of observational learning truly break free of behaviorism.

At the same time, Bandura's findings also ran counter to another major strain in psychology: psychoanalytic theory. According to the psychoanalytic concept of catharsis, when people are given an opportunity to safely release feelings of aggression, it relieves those feelings and reduces the impulses associated with them. Based on this theory, watching the adult model pummel the Bobo doll should have drained the children's aggressive feelings and reduced their violent behavior. In fact, it had the opposite effect. Bandura's studies soundly refuted the notion that watching aggressive behavior might offer a healthy catharsis for the observers.

Social learning

Main points Before Bandura, psychologist Julian Rotter had put forth his own theory of social learning. In a 1954 book, titled *Social Learning and Clinical Psychology,* Rotter held that people choose which behaviors to perform based on two factors: reinforcement value and outcome expectancy. Reinforcement value refers to the degree to which an individual values the expected reinforcement, or reward, for an action. Outcome expectancy refers to how strongly the individual expects the action to have a positive result. Clearly, Rotter laid the groundwork for much of Bandura's thinking. He also served as a crucial bridge between behaviorism and Bandura's more modern version of social learning theory.

In his theory, Bandura stressed the importance of observational learning and modeling. However, like Rotter, he also emphasized the role of expected outcomes. Bandura held that, even when people have observed and learned how to perform a behavior, they will only actually do it if they believe their action will lead to a desirable outcome.

Explanation Bandura believed that the imitation of someone else's behavior was not a passive process. Instead, it was an active choice involving four different mental functions:

- Attention—This factor was affected mainly by characteristics of the person being observed and the situation.

- Retention—This factor was affected mainly by the observer's ability to mentally process the observed behavior and store it in memory.

- Motor reproduction—This factor referred to the observer's ability to turn the stored memory into physical action. It also included the person's capacity for mentally rehearsing the behavior.

- Motivation—This factor referred to the observer's desire or drive to copy the behavior. Of all the factors, this one had the greatest influence on whether an observed behavior was actually imitated.

Bandura believed that people are capable of self-reinforcement. In other words, they can teach themselves to act in a certain way by thinking about the potential consequences of the action. Eventually, Bandura expanded this into a broader concept: self-regulation, or self-control. According to Bandura, self-regulation is the sum of a person's goals, planning, and self-reinforcement. As part of the self-regulation process, people set their own internal standards of behavior, against which they judge their own success or failure. The standards can be picked up by observational learning, and especially from watching key role models, such as parents and teachers. However, the standards can also be based on the person's own past behavior, which is used as a yardstick against which to measure future actions.

Examples Bandura studied self-regulation in several ways. For example, along with student Carol Kupers, he conducted research in which children watched either an adult or another child play a bowling game. The models had a supply of candy, from which they rewarded themselves based on either a high performance standard or a low one. Then the children who had been observing were given a chance to play the game. They, too, were provided with candy, and they were allowed to dole out their own rewards according to whatever standards they chose for themselves. Children who had watched a model set a high standard were more likely to adopt a strict standard as well. The reverse was true for children who had watched a model set a low standard.

Bandura has always been interested not only in theory, but also in practice. Based on his research, he developed the use of modeling as a therapeutic tool. Modeling has been used most often in the treatment of phobias, or irrationally intense fears. The client watches a model come into contact with the feared object, then is encouraged to imitate the model's behavior. At first, this is done under relatively nonthreatening conditions. As therapy progresses, though, the threat level is gradually raised. Eventually, the client confronts the feared object on his or her own.

Social learning and aggression

Main points Aggression is one of the most troubling, yet pervasive, aspects of human existence. It is no wonder, then, that a number of theories about the nature and causes of aggression have been proposed over the years. For example, Sigmund Freud explained aggression as a death wish that is turned outward onto others through a process called displacement. Dollard, Miller, and their colleagues proposed that aggression is a response to the frustration of some goal-directed behavior. And several ethologists who studied animal behavior, such as Konrad Lorenz, have argued that aggression is a natural instinct common to both humans and other animals.

Among these many theories, Bandura's theory of aggression as a socially learned behavior remains one of the most influential. In his early work with Walters, Bandura found that very aggressive teenagers often came from homes where the parents modeled hostile attitudes and aggressive behavior. Even when the parents would not tolerate aggression at home, they often demanded it of their sons when settling disputes with other boys. The parents were hostile toward both the school system, and the students who were blamed for harassing their sons. To Bandura, it seemed clear that the teenagers in these families were imitating the hostility and aggression of the parents.

Bandura explored this idea further in the Bobo doll studies. These studies showed the key role that observational learning plays in aggressive behavior. As Bandura later told Evans:

> If there is any behavior where observational learning is important, it is aggression, because ineffectual aggression can get one disfigured, maimed or killed. One cannot afford to learn through trial and error. So most aggressive patterns are transmitted through modeling.

Examples In the Bobo doll experiments, children watched a short film of an adult behaving violently toward the doll. The adult model not only punched the doll, but also engaged in some unusual aggressive behavior that the children were unlikely to have seen elsewhere. At one point, the model laid the doll on its side, sat on the doll, and punched it repeatedly in the nose. Then the model stood the doll back up and struck it on the head with a mallet. After that, the model threw the doll up into the air aggressively and kicked it around the room. The children were then turned loose in a playroom filled with toys, including the Bobo doll. Many who had watched the film did indeed imitate the aggressive behavior they had observed.

From this finding, it was only a short jump to wondering how media violence might be affecting millions of viewers, especially young ones. The Bobo doll studies attracted the attention of activists and politicians as well as a Presidential Commission on Violence in the Media. Bandura himself testified at congressional hearings on the subject. He also wrote about the widespread influence of media violence in a 1973 book, titled *Aggression: A Social Learning Analysis*. Bandura believed that public hearings and self-regulation by the entertainment industry were of little practical use in curbing media violence. Instead, he championed the cause of viewer demand for less violent alternatives.

In the early years of the twenty-first century, the effect of television has only become more pervasive. Its global reach has changed the world in many ways—not least of which, by greatly increasing the kinds of behaviors that children have a chance to observe. As Bandura wrote in an article in *European Psychologist*:

> In the past, modeling influences were largely confined to the styles of behavior and social practices in one's immediate community. The advent of television vastly expanded the range of models to which members of society are exposed day in and day out. By drawing on these modeled patterns of thought and behavior, observers transcend the bounds of their customary environment.

Explanation Of course, not everyone who grows up with an aggressive parent or who watches a violent television show goes on to copy what he or she has seen. According to Bandura, there are two major triggers for aggression. One is stress, or frustration, as it is called in Dollard and Miller's theory. However, Bandura notes that stress produces general emotional arousal, not a specific drive to act in a certain way. Some people may express that arousal through aggression, but others may express it by asking for help, becoming withdrawn, or escaping through alcohol or drugs. And still others use the arousal to motivate themselves to take positive steps.

The other major trigger for aggression is the expectation of benefits. This explains why some people behave aggressively even when they are not emotionally aroused. For example, some children learn that, if they act like bullies, the other children will let them have their way. Therefore, aggression can serve many purposes. As Bandura put it:

> Some people will resort to aggression to get material benefits. Others behave aggressively because it gains them status and social approval. Still others rely on aggressive conquests to build their self-esteem and sense of manliness. Some people derive satisfaction from seeing pain inflicted on those they hate. And in many instances, people resort to aggression to terminate mistreatment.

Social-cognitive theory

Main points Bandura's work on self-regulation shed new light on how people understand their own motivations and control their own actions. It also aroused Bandura's interest in how people exercise control over the nature and quality of their own lives—a capacity he refers to as human agency. Writing in the *Annual Review of Psychology,* Bandura explained the concept of agency this way: "To be an agent is to intentionally make things happen by one's actions." This capacity involves not only self-regulatory skills, but also other abilities and belief systems that play a role in self-directed change. It allows people to adapt to changing circumstances, and it gives them a means of self-development and self-renewal.

In Bandura's view, agency has certain core features that cut to the very heart of what it means to be human:

- Intentionality—Agency refers to acts that are done intentionally, and this implies the ability to make future plans.

- Forethought—In addition to making plans, people think about the future in other ways. They set goals, anticipate the likely consequences of different actions, and choose a course of action that is likely to produce positive consequences and avoid negative ones.

- Self-reactiveness—Once people have formed an intention and created an action plan, they still have to put the plan in motion. Therefore, people also must be able to motivate themselves and regulate their own behavior.

- Self-reflectiveness—People are not only agents of action, but also of thought. They have the ability to reflect on their own thoughts, motivations, and values as well as the meaning of their lives.

Giving an address as honorary president of the Canadian Psychological Association, Bandura explained why human agency holds such an important place in his social-cognitive theory:

People have the power to influence what

they do and to make things happen. They are not just onlooking hosts of brain mechanisms orchestrated by environmental events. The sensory, motor, and cerebral systems are tools people can use to accomplish things that give meaning, direction, and satisfaction to their lives.

Explanation In the 1980s, Bandura gathered all the diverse strands from his earlier research into a single theory, which he dubbed social-cognitive theory. This theory sees human functioning as the dynamic interplay of personal, environmental, and behavioral factors. (Personal factors include an individual's beliefs, thoughts, feelings, and physical responses.) Each of the three factors influences the others and is influenced by them in turn. Therefore, people are not only products of their environment, but also producers of it.

This broader view of human functioning led Bandura to realize that there might be wider possibilities for promoting change. Within the social-cognitive view, a change at any point in the three-part system can lead to changes in the other parts. The implication is that a therapy or social program can be aimed at a variety of targets and still succeed. It can be aimed at instilling positive beliefs, thoughts, feelings, and motivations. *Or,* it can be aimed at decreasing undesirable behaviors and increasing desirable ones. *Or,* it can be aimed at changing the social conditions under which people live, work, and go to school. In other words, there is more than one path to the same destination.

Examples Consider the example of an educational program aimed at improving the academic performance of students. Teachers might address personal factors by encouraging a positive attitude toward school and instilling a realistic sense of confidence in the students. They might address behavioral factors by teaching students the academic skills and good work habits that are needed to do well in school. Or, they might address environmental factors by asking the school board for funds to buy better books and supplies.

In recent years, the trend in psychology has been to shy away from grand, comprehensive theories. Bandura's social-cognitive theroy is a notable exception to the rule. By bucking the trend, Bandura has set himself apart, drawn attention to his ideas, and left his mark on fields ranging from psychology and education to healthcare and business. As he told Evans, "I have tried to analyze human lives from a broader social perspective that transcends the arbitrary boundaries of academic disciplines."

Self-efficacy

Main points The centerpiece of social-cognitive theory is self-efficacy. Bandura defines perceived self-efficacy as people's beliefs about their capability to produce desired results through their own actions. According to Bandura, people with a high sense of self-efficacy approach difficult tasks as challenges to be met, rather than threats to be avoided. They also set challenging goals for themselves, and they maintain a strong commitment to achieving them. When faced with a setback, they quickly recover their confidence and simply redouble their efforts. Bandura states that this type of outlook leads to personal successes while reducing stress and decreasing the risk of depression.

In contrast, people with a low sense of self-efficacy avoid difficult tasks, which they view as personal threats. They rarely push themselves to excel, and they have a weak commitment to any goals they do decide to pursue. When faced with an obstacle, they dwell on their personal weaknesses and the potential for failure rather than looking for solutions. If a setback occurs, they are quick to give up and slow to recover their confidence afterward. It takes relatively little for such individuals to lose faith in themselves. As a result, they easily fall prey to stress and depression.

In an article in *European Psychologist,* Bandura explained why self-efficacy beliefs are so crucial to his social-cognitive theory:

> Among the mechanisms of self-regulation none is more central or pervasive than beliefs of personal efficacy. This belief system is the foundation of human agency. Unless people believe they can produce desired outcomes and forestall undesired ones by

their actions they have little incentive to act or to persevere in the face of difficulties. Whatever other factors serve as guides and motivators, they are rooted in the core belief that one has the power to produce changes by one's actions.

Explanation According to Bandura, people's motivations, thoughts, feelings, and actions often have more to do with what they believe than with what is really true. He posits that self-efficacy beliefs have such a strong impact because they affect four major psychological processes:

- Cognitive processes—Most courses of action are first organized in thought. Often, they revolve around setting goals. The stronger people's perceived self-efficacy, higher the goals they are apt to set for themselves, and greater their commitment to achieving them. People who think of themselves as having high efficacy also tend to imagine successful outcomes. These imagined scenes of success help them plan and rehearse the steps they need to take in order to succeed in real life. In addition, people with a strong sense of self-efficacy are better equipped than those with low self-efficacy to stay task-oriented in the face of pressures, setbacks, and failures.

- Motivational processes—There are different theories about how people motivate themselves, but all are consistent with Bandura's concept of self-efficacy. For example, in attribution theory, people keep themselves motivated by attributing failures to insufficient effort, rather than low ability. This kind of thinking is typical of people with high perceived self-efficacy. In expectancy-value theory, motivation is based on people's expectation that a given action will lead to a particular result, as well as on the value they attach to that result. People who are high in perceived self-efficacy are more likely to expect that their behavior will lead to a desirable outcome. On the other hand, people who are low in perceived self-efficacy may not go after valued goals, because they do not expect to achieve them.

- Affective processes—Affective states, or feelings, are also closely tied to perceived self-efficacy. In particular, people's beliefs about their ability to cope seem to have a significant effect on how much stress and depression they actually feel in threatening or difficult situations. People who believe they can control their own disturbing thoughts are less likely to be overwhelmed by anxious or depressed thinking. In addition, two common paths to depression are unfulfilled dreams and social isolation. People with a low sense of self-efficacy are less likely to fulfill their dreams and attain their social goals.

- Selection processes—While people can affect their environment, the environment affects them in return. Therefore, one final way in which perceived self-efficacy can help shape people's lives is by influencing the kinds of environments in which they put themselves. In a 1994 article, Bandura gave the example of perceived self-efficacy affecting career choice: "The higher the level of people's perceived self-efficacy the wider the range of career options they seriously consider, the greater their interest in them, and the better they prepare themselves educationally for the occupational pursuits they choose. . ."

Obviously, a strong belief in one's own efficacy has many benefits, based on Bandura's theory. It follows that knowing how to foster this self-belief would be very helpful. Bandura has outlined four ways in which a strong sense of self-efficacy can be developed. The first and most effective way is through mastery experiences. Simply put, past successes strengthen the belief that future success is possible, while past failures undermine it. After people become convinced they have what it takes to succeed, they are more likely to stick with their goals, even when problems arise.

A second way to build strong self-efficacy beliefs is through vicarious experience; in other words, by watching other people perform the behavior. The impact of modeling on perceived self-efficacy depends largely on how much the observer sees himself or herself as being like the model. The more similar the model and observer, greater the effect. When people watch someone similar to themselves accomplish a task through sustained effort, they are more likely to believe that they can do it, too. At the same time, they may learn some of the skills they need to succeed by observing the successful model. On the other hand, when people see someone fail despite great effort, they are more likely to lose faith in their own abilities as well.

A third way to instill self-efficacy beliefs is by social persuasion; that is, by telling people that they can be successful. People who are persuaded by others that they have what it takes to succeed are likely to try harder and be more persistent than those who hold self-doubts. Unfortunately, it is much harder to build up perceived self-efficacy this way than it is to destroy it. Unrealistically positive messages may be quickly disproved, leading to failure and demoralization. On the other hand, overly negative messages may keep people from achieving as much as they could, by persuading them not to attempt a challenging task in the first place or by convincing them to give up at the first sign of difficulty.

A final way that self-efficacy beliefs are reinforced is through emotional and physiological reactions. When people face a stressful or challenging situation, they naturally experience emotional and physiological arousal. Those who are high in perceived self-efficacy may see this arousal as a sign that they are energized. The energetic feeling, in turn, helps them perform their best, which adds to their sense of self-efficacy in the future. In contrast, people who are low in perceived self-efficacy may see arousal as a sign of stress they are helpless to control. The situation can quickly turn into a self-fulfilling prophesy. For example, athletes who view arousal before a game as a sign of fear or weakness are unlikely to play their best. The poor performance, in turn, further lowers their sense of self-efficacy.

In sum, Bandura contends that perceived self-efficacy is critical to success in almost any area. As he wrote in his 1994 article, "the successful, the venturesome, the sociable, the nonanxious, the nondepressed, the social reformers, and the innovators take an optimistic view of their personal capabilities to exercise influence over events that affect their lives. If not unrealistically exaggerated, such self-beliefs foster positive well-being and human accomplishments."

Examples Everyday life is filled with obstacles and difficulties. Bandura believes that people need a strong sense of self-efficacy in order to take on a challenge or keep plugging away when problems arise. He notes that when people vastly overestimate their own abilities, this can lead to trouble. However, people may need a somewhat optimistic view of themselves in order to achieve great things. As Bandura wrote in a 1994 article: "If efficacy beliefs always reflected only what people can do routinely they would rarely fail but they would not set aspirations beyond their immediate reach nor mount the extra effort needed to surpass their ordinary performances."

High perceived self-efficacy can help people keep trying in the face of setbacks. As an example of this, Bandura cites a number of great authors, artists, musicians, and scientists who met with early rejection, including James Joyce, Vincent Van Gogh, Igor Stravinsky, and Robert Goddard. Without a strong belief in their own capability to achieve something worthwhile through their actions, these individuals might have given up early in their careers, and the world would have been the poorer for it.

Bandura claims that groups of people can hold beliefs about their collective self-efficacy as well. He says that the strength of organizations and even whole nations lies partly in the members' belief that they can improve their lives through their combined efforts. Without this belief, people may not choose to work as a group, or they may not put much effort into it. They also may not have the determination to stick with their goals if their joint efforts fail to produce fast results.

How do different people come to see themselves as having more or less self-efficacy? According to Bandura, people's experiences at key points in life can affect the development of their perceived self-efficacy. These are not firm stages that everyone must pass through, however. Instead, they are merely typical experiences that help shape many people's views of their own abilities and limitations.

- Infancy—Newborns have no sense of self, according to Bandura. However, as babies grow, they gradually develop an awareness of their ability to produce effects by their own actions. They shake a rattle to make a sound, for instance, or cry to bring Mom into the room. Babies who get reliable results from their actions start to become more and more attuned to their own behavior and its effects. At the same time, babies become increasingly aware of their separateness from other people. Eventually, they form an abstract idea of themselves as a distinct self.

- Childhood and families—Young children continue to test their abilities and learn from the results they get. At this early age, children are adding new physical, mental, social, and language skills almost daily. If they are able to put these new skills to good use, then they develop a sense of self-efficacy. Bandura believes that parents can encourage this process by being responsive to their babies' behavior and providing a safe but rich environment for trying out the new skills. For example, a toddler might learn that every time he says "Momma, look," Mom appears and takes a few minutes to talk to him. Or, a young child might learn that she is able to create fascinating, colorful patterns by moving a crayon across a sheet of paper. From these kinds of daily experiences, children learn that they have the power to control some of the things that occur in their world.

- Childhood and peers—As children grow, they begin to learn from and compare themselves to other children. Older children may serve as role models, while children of the same age provide a standard against which youngsters can compare their own abilities. Because peers serve as important influences, a lack of interaction with siblings and friends can interfere with the development of perceived self-efficacy.

- Childhood and school—As children reach school age, school becomes the main place in which they acquire and test their mental abilities. These abilities are learned not only through formal education, but also from observing how other students use their thinking skills. Several factors affect how children come to see their own abilities. These factors include comparisons to other students, comments from teachers, rewards for progress, and the satisfaction of achieving goals.

- Adolescence—The teen years are a period of rapid change. Teenagers need a strong sense of self-efficacy to handle all the physical, mental, and social changes in their lives. Tricky new issues may arise, such as decisions about drug use and sexual behavior. According to Bandura, teenagers who are overly sheltered from making these kinds of choices may not have a chance to learn good decision-making skills. On the other hand, teenagers with a weak sense of self-efficacy may not be prepared to stand up to peer pressure. During these years, teenagers also must get ready for the challenges of adulthood that lie ahead. This means they need to master a whole new set of skills for living in adult society. In addition, they must make important choices about college and career, and their beliefs about their own abilities are likely to have a big impact on the choices they make.

- Early adulthood—As young adults, people need to cope with many new demands, including marriage, parenthood, and career. A firm sense of self-efficacy can help them master the skills they need. On the other hand, those who see themselves as low in self-efficacy are likely to find that they are plagued by self-doubts and ill-equipped to tackle new challenges. As a result, they may fall victim to stress and depression.

- Middle age—In middle adulthood, people tend to settle into stable routines, which helps them solidify their sense of self-efficacy in key areas of their lives. However, the apparent stability is an illusion. It is always balanced by the need to keep up with changes in society. At work, there is constant pressure from younger competitors. Even in middle age, then, people need to keep growing and learning. A strong belief in their own efficacy helps them accomplish this growth.

- Late adulthood—The major issues of late life often revolve around retirement, illness, and the loss of loved ones. As in earlier years, a firm sense of self-efficacy helps. For example, people with high perceived self-efficacy are better prepared to take up a new hobby or make new friends after retirement. In addition, older adults with a strong sense of self-efficacy are less likely to exaggerate the decline in abilities that occurs with age. In contrast, those with low perceived self-efficacy are apt to see every small problem as a sign that they are going downhill fast. This belief may keep them from fully enjoying the last years of their lives.

A quick survey of any psychology journal from just a few years ago will reveal that many of the studies and theories published in these journals are already outdated. Yet Bandura's work over the span of more than 40 years has remained remarkably fresh and timely. His first important research dealt with modeling and aggression. Much of his more recent work deals with the development and importance of self-efficacy beliefs in a variety of settings. Both lines of research are still very active and relevant areas of study—a tribute to Bandura's skill as both researcher and theorist.

Social-cognitive theory and moral disengagement

Main points Bandura began his career by studying aggression in children and teenagers. Near the end of his career, the roots of aggression and violence are still of great interest to him. He has extended his research to include all kinds of moral disengagement; in other words, the capacity for all types of antisocial and immoral acts. In social-cognitive theory, the capacity for self-control over moral behavior has two functions. On one hand, it gives people the ability to refrain from acting inhumanely. On the other hand, it gives people the ability to behave in a kind and sensitive manner.

According to Bandura, people set standards for themselves that guide their moral behavior. Most of the time, these standards help people keep themselves in line. People refrain from behaving badly, because that would bring self-blame and guilt. Instead, they usually prefer to act in a way that leaves them with a sense of worth and self-respect. Sometimes, however, people use tricks of thinking to let themselves off the hook for violating their own standards.

Explanation The kinds of thoughts that lead to moral disengagement include:

- Moral justification—To make bad conduct seem more acceptable, people tell themselves that it serves a worthy purpose.

- Euphemistic labeling—When discussing offensive or upsetting behavior, people avoid describing it bluntly and instead substitute harmless-sounding terms.

- Advantageous comparison—To make vile acts seem less reprehensible, people compare them to even worse behavior.

- Displacement of responsibility—To avoid personal responsibility for their actions, people view themselves as just following orders.

- Diffusion of responsibility—To reduce their own responsibility for an act, people share the labor and focus on just their part of it, which seems harmless by itself.

- Disregard or distortion of consequences— When people hurt others, they think about the consequences in ways that ignore or minimize the harm.

- Dehumanization—To justify inhumane behavior, people view the victims as being less than human.

- Attribution of blame—To excuse cruel or violent behavior, people blame it on the victims.

Fortunately, just as people can use their

thoughts to justify immorality, they can also use them to motivate moral behavior. As Bandura sees it, moral thinking helps stop immoral actions in part by helping people control their angry feelings. Anger control, in turn, is based partly on people's belief in their ability to handle their emotions; in other words, on their perceived self-efficacy for emotional control.

Social factors also play a big role in moral behavior. Problems can arise when there is a conflict between the moral standards people set for themselves and the standards of society. At times, people may find themselves being pressured by others to follow courses of action that are at odds with their own moral code. The response to this kind of pressure depends on the relative strength of the personal and social forces. In some cases, a moral tug-of-war can produce principled dissent and social activism. In other cases, however, it may lead to moral disengagement.

Examples In recent years, Bandura has studied how people reach the point of moral disengagement. For example, in one study, Bandura and three colleagues from the University of Rome studied 799 Italian students in the sixth through eighth grades. The students filled out several questionnaires designed to assess their moral disengagement as well as other relevant aspects of their thoughts, feelings, and behaviors. The researchers found that students who reported lots of morally disengaged thinking did indeed tend to commit more aggressive and antisocial acts.

Compared to students with a strong sense of morality, those who were morally disengaged also tended to be easily angered. In addition, they were prone to thinking about revenge for past slights. These feelings and thoughts just added to their propensity for aggression. When the morally disengaged students did act aggressively, they were not much bothered by guilt. They also did not feel the need to make amends for any harm they had caused.

The flip side is that morally oriented thinking can prevent many aggressive and antisocial acts. People who take personal responsibility for their actions are less likely to behave badly, even when provoked. When such people have an aggressive impulse, one way they keep themselves from acting on it is through self-reproof. And if they occasionally fail to keep their behavior in check, such people try to make amends to those they have hurt.

In these dangerous times, exploring ways to promote a more humane society seems like a particularly important use of social-cognitive theory. In Bandura's words, "At the social level, we need to create control mechanisms so that social systems support compassionate behavior rather than inhumane activities."

HISTORICAL CONTEXT

On an Emory University website devoted to Bandura, there is a page that traces Bandura's "professional genealogy" back through six previous generations of psychologists. The line of descent goes like this:

- William James influenced
- James Rowland Angell at Harvard University, who influenced
- John Watson at the University of Chicago, who influenced
- Karl Spencer Lashley at Johns Hopkins University, who influenced
- Carney Landis at the University of Minnesota, who influenced
- Art Benton at Columbia University, who influenced
- Albert Bandura at the University of Iowa

POSITIVE		NEGATIV
REINFORCEMENT		
The frequency	When a person receives	When a person experiences a

of a behavior is increased because of the behavior of the subject.	reinforcement after engaging in some behavior, the person is likely to repeat that behavior.	negative state an does something t eliminate the undesired state, t person is likely t repeat that behavior.
PUNISHMENT		
The frequency of a behavior is decreased because of the behavior of the subject.	When a person engages in a behavior and something negative is applied as a result, that behavior is less likely to be repeated.	When a person engages in a behavior and something positi is taken away, th behavior is less likely to be repeated.

(Courtesy Thomson Gale.)

Although this is a lighthearted exercise, it has a serious point: No scientist works in isolation. All scientists, including Bandura, are heavily influenced by the work of those who have gone before. In some cases, Bandura built upon the ideas of his predecessors. In other cases, he reacted against an idea by proposing an alternative.

Hull, Spence, and behaviorism

At the time Bandura was in graduate school, psychology was dominated by behaviorism, a theory that holds that people can be conditioned to respond in specific ways to specific stimuli. According to strict behaviorism, people's personalities are nothing more than the sum total of the behaviors learned through this conditioning process. Thus, with complete understanding of stimuli and responses, it should be possible to predict and control the behavior of individuals and even entire cultures.

One of the central concepts of behaviorism is reinforcement. Simply put, this is an event that strengthens a behavior and makes it more likely to be repeated in the future. Positive reinforcement produces pleasant feelings, while negative reinforcement relieves unpleasant feelings. Either way, the person feels better after performing the behavior. Punishment, on the other hand, is an event that decreases the likelihood that a behavior will be repeated in the future. It produces this effect by making the person feel worse after performing the behavior. Although punishment may make a behavior less likely in the short term, it is usually not a good way to get rid of a behavior permanently. In general, its impact on behavior is not as powerful as that of reinforcement. As the saying goes, you can catch more flies with honey than with vinegar.

In its purest form, behaviorism implies that behavior is nothing more than a function of stimuli, rewards, and punishments. By the 1930s and '40s, however, a number of experimental psychologists were already starting to chafe at this notion. While they still believed that external events were paramount, they also thought it was important to consider internal states. Hull, a professor at Yale University, was one of the most influential of these new-style behaviorists.

Hull did most of his research in white rats, rather than humans. Like other behaviorists, he believed that it was only logical to start by studying the simpler stimuli and responses of lower animals. The information gleaned from these animals could then be used to understand complex human behaviors. Hull believed that animals made responses in order to relieve an internal drive. The responses themselves then became stimuli, leading to more responses. This explained how a rat presented with the stimulus of a maze could make a whole series of responses to find its way to food, which would reduce its hunger drive.

Hull's main contribution, however, was turning attention onto the internal state of the animal while it was learning. Other researchers built on this idea. Among them was Kenneth Spence, who had studied with Hull at Yale University. Spence believed that reinforcement was not absolutely necessary for learning to occur. However, he still thought that reinforcement was a very powerful motivator. Spence became head of the psychology department at the University of Iowa in 1942. When Bandura arrived there, Spence was still the guiding force in the department, and the University of Iowa was a major center of experimental psychology.

Thus, Bandura was immersed in behaviorism as a student. Right from the start, however, he was uncomfortable with some of its tenets. From the beginning of his research career, Bandura argued against conditioning as the main method of learning new behaviors. Instead, he argued for the importance of observational learning and modeling. Of course, Bandura did not deny that conditioning could occur, nor did he claim that rewards and punishments were completely ineffective. He simply suggested that the observation of models was a more efficient way of learning in most situations.

Bandura also stressed that, when reinforcement had an effect, it was not a mindless process. In fact, reinforcement worked by teaching people to expect positive outcomes; in other words, by affecting the way they thought about things. Therefore, while behaviorism focused on outer stimuli and responses, Bandura focused on the inner thinking that connected the two. This was the cognitive part of his social-cognitive theory.

In addition, Bandura disagreed with the behaviorist focus on the control of human behavior through outward rewards and punishments. Early on, he emphasized the power of self-regulation. He believed that people could control their own behavior by setting personal standards and rewarding themselves for meeting these self-imposed goals. Over time, this idea evolved into the broader concept of human agency, which holds that people can exercise some control over the nature and quality of events around them. As Bandura sees it, people are not just passive pawns of their environment. On the contrary, they are active directors of their own lives.

Miller, Dollard, and social learning

Miller and Dollard were also part of the group of psychologists who had gathered at Yale in the 1930s and '40s and were influenced by Hull. Miller and Dollard produced the first scholarly work on social learning. As they saw it, social learning involved habits, which were the associations between particular stimuli and responses. These habits were built up by way of a hierarchy of acquired drives. As an example, say a boy was petting a dog, when the dog suddenly attacked him. The boy would learn to avoid dogs whenever possible in the future. Beyond that, though, the boy would probably feel fear if a dog ran up to him in the park. This learned fear, in turn, would be an acquired drive that could itself lead to new behaviors that reduced the fear. For example, the boy might learn to always carry a stick for protection when walking through the park. Or, the boy might learn to wear headphones and play his favorite music. Of course, the music would not do anything to protect him from the dog, but it would reduce the acquired drive of fear.

Miller and Dollard tried to use this concept of acquired drives to show how a complex adult personality could be built up out of the simple drives and responses of a baby. For example, if a baby is regularly rewarded for smiling and cooing when being held and fed, the baby may learn to be more socially active. Over time, this could develop into an outgoing personality. Miller and Dollard stressed that children's personalities were formed through social rewards. They also allowed for inner drives and motivations. Yet ultimately, their theory was still firmly rooted in conditioning.

Bandura picked up where Miller and Dollard left off. He, too, emphasized that children learn from social situations. However, he suggested that rewards were not necessary for this to occur. Bandura also moved internal thought processes to center stage. For Miller, Dollard, and the behaviorists before them, the essence of personality was in people's behavior. For Bandura, it was in their thoughts and beliefs.

Rotter and social learning

Rotter was another graduate of the University of Iowa, where he took classes with Lewin. However, he had moved on before Bandura arrived. In 1954, Rotter published *Social Learning and Clinical Psychology,* in which he laid out his own theory of social learning. Where Miller and

Dollard's work in this area had been firmly grounded in conditioning and reinforcement, Rotter's work was a step further removed from behaviorism. Of course, this means it was also a step closer to Bandura's theory, which followed. In fact, Rotter's theory is often seen as a bridge between behaviorally based social learning theories and Bandura's cognitively based ideas.

Rotter believed that what we call personality is really an interaction between a person and the environment. Personality does not exist within a person independently of the environment in which that individual lives. By the same token, though, personality also does not consist of just a simple set of responses to stimuli. Instead, the very nature of the environment that a person responds to is affected by that individual's past learning experiences. To continue the earlier example, say the person who had been attacked by a dog in the past is walking with a friend when another dog approaches. The first person will respond with fear. However, if the friend has happy memories of a beloved childhood pet, she will probably have an entirely different response to the same dog. The difference in the two individuals' responses is based on their very different set of expectations.

According to Rotter, the way people ultimately act in a particular situation will be determined by two things: outcome expectancy, or how strongly they expect the behavior to have a positive result, and reinforcement value, or how much they value the expected reward. In the 1960s, Rotter also began looking at people's expectations about whether they could affect the rewards they received. Those who generally expected that they could achieve desired rewards through their own actions were said to have an internal locus of control. Those who believed that rewards were due to fate or luck, and therefore out of their hands, were said to have an external locus of control.

Rotter thought that reinforcement had a big influence on human behavior. However, he also recognized that people had long-lasting personal traits that were quite important as well. He identified locus of control as a trait that affected a whole range of behaviors in a number of settings. Subsequent research has shown that individuals do indeed seem to differ in locus of control, and that this difference is relatively stable over time.

It is easy to see the seeds of many of Bandura's ideas in Rotter's work. Both men stressed that behavior is the result of an interaction between the outer world and the inner thoughts of an individual. In particular, both men emphasized the importance of outcome expectations. In addition, Bandura's concept of perceived self-efficacy bears a notable similarity to Rotter's locus of control. Each of these concepts deals with people's beliefs about their ability to get the results they want through their own actions.

Sears and childhood aggression

At the time that Bandura began his career at

Stanford, Robert Sears was chairman of the psychology department there. Sears was yet another member of the group of psychologists who had been heavily influenced by Hull at Yale, and who had gone on to make their own mark in psychology. Sears was especially interested in studying child-rearing patterns. He hoped to find observable behaviors that could be tied to psychoanalytic concepts of personality development. Psychoanalytic theory, originally developed by Sigmund Freud, held that people's behavior is often the result of unconscious mental activity. According to the theory, many adult emotional problems are the result of unconscious conflicts that first arose during critical stages of emotional development in childhood.

In an effort to find the childhood sources of dependency and aggression, Sears compared children's personality traits to their mothers' child-rearing practices. There were some flaws in the way Sears designed his study. For one thing, he relied on the mothers' self-reports of their practices, which may not have been accurate. Nevertheless, Sears found that more use of punishment by the mothers was related to higher levels of both dependency and aggression in the children.

Sears was only one of many psychologists at the time who were looking for a way to reconcile behaviorism, with its total focus on external behavior, and psychoanalytic theory, with its opposite focus on internal experience. For example, Dollard and Miller had also suggested that many emotional disorders might be conditioned responses to parental punishments. This idea received at least partial support in Sears's research.

Like Sears, Bandura was interested in exploring the childhood roots of aggressive behavior. However, Sears believed that parents influenced their children to become more aggressive through the use of punishments. Bandura, on the other hand, stressed that parents were role models for their children, who learned to behave aggressively mainly by imitation.

Television and aggression

In the early 1960s, Bandura was just publishing the results of his Bobo doll experiments. At about the same time, television was in the midst of a great boom. In 1945, there were probably fewer than 10,000 TV sets in the entire United States. By 1960, that figure had soared to almost 60 million. Along with TV's explosive growth in popularity, there was also an increase in criticism of the programs that were offered. Critics accused the TV networks of promoting antisocial and aggressive behavior by bringing a steady stream of violence into American homes.

As public debate began to heat up, researchers started to look for links between televised violence and the real thing. Bandura's research on modeling and aggression in children dovetailed nicely with this trend. As with other behaviors, Bandura stressed that merely observing violence and aggression on TV did not necessarily translate into copying it. Yet sometimes it did, occasionally with tragic consequences. As Bandura told Evans,

> I draw the important distinction between the power of the media to produce learning and its power to affect action. The learning effects are rather uniform. If children watch one hundred ways of killing people hundreds of times they will learn one hundred ways to kill people. But the effects on action are variable. We need to explain the conditions under which people are going to act on what they have learned.

A number of researchers have taken up this challenge. It has been estimated that more than 3,000 studies have now attempted to look for the links between televised and real-life violence. Nevertheless, it is still unclear exactly how TV exerts its effects on vulnerable individuals. In general, though, research has shown that children who are exposed to TV violence are more likely to behave aggressively. In addition, they may become less sensitive to the pain and suffering of others, and they may be more fearful of the outside world.

Humanistic psychology

Around the time that Bandura came on the scene, other psychologists were starting to rebel against the confines of strict behaviorism as well. In particular, many were dissatisfied with behaviorism's focus on observable behavior. Instead, they preferred to focus on inner experience, mental processes, and people's concept of self. In the 1960s, this led to the rise of the humanistic movement in psychology.

Humanists rejected the behaviorist view that people's behavior is nothing more than a set of responses to environmental stimuli. They felt that this took the humanity out of human behavior, reducing people to the level of machines. At the same time, humanists also rejected the psychoanalytic view that a selfish desire for pleasure was at the heart of all human behavior. Rather, the humanists emphasized the innate potential of people and their ability to exercise control over their own destinies.

The self is a central concept in humanistic psychology. Carl Rogers, one of the leaders of the movement, believed that behavior problems were the result of people's failure to trust their own experience, which led to a distorted view of the self. The goal of therapy was to reduce this distortion by helping people gain self-understanding and self-acceptance. Abraham Maslow, another key figure in humanistic psychology, wrote about people's innate drive to achieve self-actualization—a process of inner growth in which they realized their potential.

While not a humanistic psychologist, Bandura is also very interested in the self. He has written about something he calls the self-system—a set of cognitive processes that people use to perceive, evaluate, and control their own behavior. This self-system allows people to adapt their behavior so that it is appropriate for the situation at hand and effective for helping them achieve their goals.

Cognitive psychology

Another movement in psychology undoubtedly played a big role in shaping Bandura's opinions. In the 1950s, cognitive psychology began moving to the forefront of research and theory. This branch of psychology sees human perception and thought processes as being central to the human experience. Cognitive, or thought, processes can involve language, symbols, or imagery. Such processes include perceiving, recognizing, evaluating, imagining, and remembering information. They are essential for attention, reasoning, planning, problem solving, and decision making.

There are several reasons why cognitive psychology became so popular in the mid-twentieth century. One was the growing dissatisfaction with behaviorism. Another was the advent of modern linguistics, which shed new light on how people learn and use language. Yet another was the birth of computer science, which led scientists to ponder the difference between human thought and machine "intelligence." Around the same time, developmental psychologists such as Jean Piaget aroused new interest in the way human mental abilities unfold as children mature. Meanwhile, innovative research on verbal learning and memory gave rise to fresh insights about how memory works.

All of these developments helped focus attention on the crucial role of thought processes. Of course, such processes are at the core of Bandura's ideas about how people learn and function. In fact, he renamed his theory social-*cognitive* theory to emphasize that very point. As Bandura wrote in *Social Foundations of Thought and Action*: "A theory that denies that thoughts can regulate actions does not lend itself readily to the explanation of complex human behavior."

Bandura's ideas have met with wide acceptance and have been very influential. Like any strong leader, Bandura has inspired many followers. However, he has also attracted his share of challengers and critics. In fact, it is largely through give-and-take with colleagues and competitors that scientific theories such as Bandura's are refined over the years.

Newer cognitive approaches

As its name implies, social-cognitive theory is at its best when it comes to describing social and cognitive factors. It does a particularly good job of explaining the social situations in which complex behaviors are learned and the cognitive processes by which people decide whether or not to imitate those behaviors. Bandura and his followers argue that cognitive processes are especially important to study and understand, because they capture the very essence of what it means to be human.

Social-cognitive theory arose as a reaction to behaviorism and, to a lesser extent, psychoanalytic theory. Bandura was very successful at breaking free from these earlier viewpoints. Yet critics argue that the pendulum may have swung too far in the opposite direction. Some claim that social-cognitive theory goes too far in downplaying the role of reinforcement and conditioning in affecting behavior. Others complain that the theory ignores the emotional and unconscious aspects of personality.

Still other critics fault social-cognitive theory for oversimplifying cognition as well. In recent decades, cognitive psychology has been strongly influenced by technological advances in both computer science and neuroscience. This combination of cognitive psychology and neuroscience has given birth to a brand-new field: cognitive neuroscience. The hybrid field attempts to unite the study of the mind with the study of the brain. It looks at both psychological and physiological aspects of memory, sensation, perception, problem solving, language, motor functions, and thought. There is even a subspecialty called social-cognitive neuroscience, which looks specifically at the mind/brain processes involved in social learning and interpersonal communication.

There are several reasons why cognitive neuroscience has taken off so quickly. One is the development of sophisticated brain imaging techniques, such as positron emission tomography (PET) and functional magnetic resonance imaging (fMRI). These techniques allow scientists to peer into the human brain and observe it in action as never before. For the first time, the goal of identifying specific brain pathways linked to particular thoughts, feelings, and behaviors seems more like science than science fiction. It is little wonder that scientists are excited. Today, many are trying to develop psychological models of thought processes that are consistent with what is known about the structure and function of the nervous system.

It could be argued that a cognitive theory without a solid foundation in neuroscience is a bit old-fashioned in this high-tech age. Yet cognitive neuroscience is still in its infancy, and research has a long way to go before it comes close to fully describing how a thought is formed or how memory is stored. Even if it becomes possible someday to break down a single thought into a detailed series of connections within the brain, however, this still would not explain how the overall system of connections works. More importantly, it would not show how that system translates into thought, emotion, or individual personality.

Defining the terms

Another point raised by some critics is that Bandura's concepts are not as precisely defined as they could be. As a result, there is some room for ambiguity. While this might be fine in everyday life, it is a serious problem in science, where the goal is to be as precise and accurate as possible.

In an article in *American Psychologist,* William Powers outlined concerns about Bandura's use of the word "belief" in a variety of contexts:

> Bandura spoke of belief in ways that sometimes seem to mean a kind of goal (as in a belief that one is justified in

setting high goals), at other times seem to describe perceptions (beliefs about one's actual effectiveness in achieving a given goal), and at still others suggest imagination (rehearsing or imagining achieving a goal without actually behaving.

Powers noted that the role played by a belief in affecting behavior would be different, depending on which of these meanings was intended.

Critics have also charged that some of Bandura's terms are just new labels given to existing concepts. For example, Bandura's self-efficacy is similar to Rotter's locus of control. Not surprisingly, research has indicated that there is some overlap between the two concepts, based on statistical comparisons of people's scores on tests of both.

However, this does not mean the two concepts are identical. In a 1991 article, Bandura explained the difference this way:

Perceived self-efficacy is concerned with people's beliefs about their capabilities to organize and execute designated courses of action. Locus of control refers to people's beliefs that outcomes are dependent on their actions or are the result of chance, fate, or luck. Beliefs about whether one can produce certain performances cannot, by any stretch of the imagination, be considered the same as beliefs about whether actions affect outcomes.

Bandura's focus on outcome expectations is also similar to Rotter's outcome expectancy and reinforcement value. In a 2003 article with Edwin Locke, Bandura explained the difference as he sees it:

> In expectancy-value theory, motivation is governed by the expectation that given performances will produce particular outcomes and the value individuals place on the expected outcomes. However, people act on their beliefs about what they can do as well as their beliefs about the likely outcomes of performance.

Bandura notes that people may rule out behaviors on self-efficacy grounds without bothering to think about the expected costs and benefits. For example, a student who sees himself as having low math self-efficacy might rule out signing up for an advanced math class before even considering how much work the class would require or whether it would help him get into college.

Power of self-efficacy

None of Bandura's ideas has had broader appeal than the concept of self-efficacy. A search of PsycINFO database, the APA's bibliographic listing of the psychological literature, found 3,453 journal articles with "self-efficacy" as the subject published from 1974 through 2003. Dozens of questionnaires for assessing specific kinds of self-efficacy have been developed for use in such studies. The particular types of beliefs that researchers have tried to study include self-efficacy for academic achievement, alcohol abstinence, arthritis self-care, chronic disease management, computer use, controlling eating habits, diabetes self-care, dissertation completion, drinking refusal, driving, foreign language learning, exercise, Internet teaching, leisure time skills, mathematics, meeting others' expectations, occupational skills, problem solving, science laboratory skills, self-assertiveness, self-directed learning, social interactions, teaching, and writing, to name just a few.

As with any concept that is so widely used, the results have varied in their nature and quality. However, a substantial literature now exists on the role of self-efficacy beliefs in educational and occupational success. Numerous studies have also looked at the importance of perceived self-efficacy in determining whether people adopt healthy behaviors and how well they manage the symptoms of chronic illness when it occurs. Beyond this, Bandura has also discussed the collective efficacy of groups.

One key question is whether self-efficacy beliefs really have as much impact on behavior as Bandura claims. Bandura makes a strong case that they do. In a 2003 article, he points out that this question has now been addressed using a wide variety of study designs and statistical techniques.

Nine large meta-analyses—statistical analyses that combine the results of several studies—have also been done. These meta-analyses looked at diverse topics, including self-efficacy for work performance, social functioning, academic achievement, and sports performance. They involved children, teenagers, and adults. Some included laboratory studies where self-efficacy beliefs were altered experimentally, while others included studies of self-efficacy in real life. Two meta-analyses looked at the perceived efficacy of groups of people working together.

Bandura sums up the findings this way: "The evidence from these meta-analyses is consistent in showing that efficacy beliefs contribute significantly to the level of motivation and performance." Studies have shown that groups of people with different levels of perceived self-efficacy tend to behave differently. In addition, studies have shown that it is often possible to predict behavior changes within individuals as their self-efficacy beliefs change over time. The fact that so many different kinds of studies using different designs have found evidence for the power of self-efficacy makes Bandura's claims that much more convincing.

Of course, not every study has yielded positive results. Also, critics have noted that many of the studies that found a positive link between self-efficacy beliefs and behavior had a correlational design. This type of study can show the degree of association between two variables, but it cannot show whether one caused the other. Some studies with experimental designs, which do indicate a causal effect, have found support for Bandura's theory. However, others have not, and a few have even found that high perceived self-efficacy was related to worse, not better, performance on a task. Overall, however, the research seems to support the usefulness of self-efficacy beliefs.

Accuracy of self-beliefs

Bandura has argued that it may be most helpful if people's judgments of their own efficacy slightly exceed their current ability level. This slight overestimation may push people to increase their effort and ultimately improve their skills. However, it seems likely that there is a point where confidence becomes overconfidence, and it starts to hurt rather than help people's performance. Such overconfidence might push people to keep setting unrealistic goals and attempting tasks for which they are completely unprepared. This kind of mismatch between people's beliefs and their true ability is almost certain to lead to failure. One issue that researchers still need to clarify, then, is the point where high self-efficacy beliefs become *too* high.

This is a real concern for managers, teachers, therapists, and others who are interested in helping people develop useful self-efficacy beliefs. Few experts would suggest devising programs or therapies specifically to lower people's sense of self-efficacy. However, it may be just as bad to try to overinflate people's notions of what they can do. A better alternative may be to help people understand exactly what they do and do not know, so that they can more effectively choose how to approach a particular task.

While some people tend to overestimate their own efficacy, others are prone to underestimation. One well-known example is the difference between male and female students. Girls, on average, perform as well as boys on a variety of academic tasks. However, girls often see themselves as less academically capable, and this gap just widens the longer they are in school. This belief may translate into choosing less challenging classes, ruling out areas of study without even trying them, putting less effort in excelling, or giving up too quickly when problems arise. Therefore, it is clearly just as important for teachers and others to provide a reality check when self-beliefs are too low as when they are too high.

Self-efficacy and explanatory style

Cognitive psychology continues to evolve. As already noted, one research-oriented branch has merged with neuroscience. Another branch, with closer ties to clinical practice, has turned its attention to the cognitive styles that characterize different people. Explanatory style is the name usually given to the set of cognitive variables that describe how a person habitually interprets the events in his or her life. One example of an explanatory style is optimism versus pessimism. Although optimism is different from high perceived self-efficacy, the two concepts have some features in common.

Martin Seligman has been a leading figure in this area. In the 1960s and '70s, he conducted studies in which he showed how animals could develop learned helplessness. In a classic set of experiments, Seligman gave unpleasant electric shocks to dogs, who were restrained so that they could not avoid or escape the shocks. Later, the restraints were removed, and the dogs were given shocks again. The dogs tended to stay in place and suffer the consequences, even though they could have easily escaped. It was as if the dogs had given up trying to help themselves. Research with people has shown similar results. If people learn that they have no control over their situation, they tend to stop trying to accomplish much, even when it might be within their power. Over time, this can lead to depression, stress, and apathy.

More recently, Seligman has written about learned optimism and pessimism. As Seligman describes them, pessimists tend to believe that bad events will last a long time, undermining whatever they do. They also think that these bad events are their own fault. Optimists, in contrast, have the opposite reaction when faced with the same hard knocks. They tend to see problems as just temporary setbacks with limited effects. They also believe the problems are not their fault. Instead, the problems are blamed on circumstances, bad luck, or other people—not their own lack of capability. When faced with a tough situation, optimists see it as a challenge and redouble their efforts to succeed.

Seligman's is only one of several theories that look at how people explain successes and failures. These theories, like Bandura's theory of self-efficacy, attempt to show what motivates people to act. However, explanatory styles, such as optimism or pessimism, tend to be generalized, affecting all areas of life. Self-efficacy beliefs, on the other hand, tend to be specific. It is quite possible for a person to see herself as high in athletic self-efficacy but low in academic self-efficacy, for instance. Yet that same person may also have a general tendency to be an optimist or pessimist in most situations most of the time.

Self-efficacy at work

A number of studies have looked at the way self-efficacy beliefs influence people's choice of career. This research has shed light on how perceived self-efficacy affect decision-making in general. In a 2003 article with Locke, Bandura summed up the findings this way:

> The findings of this substantial body of research showed that the higher the perceived self-efficacy to fulfill educational requirements and occupational roles is, the wider are the career options people seriously consider

pursuing, the greater is the interest they have in them, the better they prepare themselves educationally for different occupational careers, and the greater is their staying power in challenging career pursuits.

Occupational self-efficacy may actually become an issue long before people apply for their first job. That is because students' beliefs about their job capabilities and preferences are formed at an early age, based on studies that have looked at this subject. In one study by Bandura and his colleagues, information was gathered about a group of students when they entered junior high school. The combination of self-efficacy beliefs and social factors at that time predicted the kinds of career goals that the same students had by the end of junior high. This, in turn, might have affected whether the students took the classes they needed in order to reach their goals.

Bandura has noted that the modern workplace is demanding ever-greater self-efficacy of its workers. The highly skilled nature of many jobs today means that people must take the necessary steps to train for their careers. The fast pace of change and the constant flood of new information means that workers must take an active role to keep their skills up-to-date. Rather than settling into one job for life, most workers also need the ability to adapt to various jobs and work settings over the course of their careers.

Bandura says that collective self-efficacy is important for modern companies, too. Companies have to adapt to a rapidly changing global marketplace. They need to keep up with the latest technologies as well. A sense of self-efficacy as a group may be a key ingredient of long-term success, if it allows the company to successfully adapt and innovate.

Self-efficacy at school

In a knowledge-based society, school is more important than ever before. According to self-efficacy theory, the beliefs that students hold about themselves are vital factors in their success or failure at school. Such beliefs may influence why students pick some classes and activities and avoid others. Self-efficacy beliefs also may affect whether students make the necessary effort to succeed. In addition, differences in self-efficacy beliefs may explain why some students are enthusiastic and confident, while others who are equally talented are filled with dread and panic whenever they have to give a presentation or take a test.

Several studies have now looked at perceived self-efficacy in math and science. Not surprisingly, the studies have shown that college students tend to choose college majors and career fields in which they feel most competent, and to avoid fields in which they feel less competent. In many cases, young women avoid math and science courses not because they lack competence, but because they underestimate their own capabilities in this area. This is a loss not only for the young women, but also for society as a whole, which needs more math- and science-trained workers.

A second group of studies have shown that teachers' beliefs about their own efficacy affect how and what they teach. This, in turn, affects what students learn in their classes. Teachers with a low sense of self-efficacy also tend to take a dim view of their students' motivation. The teachers focus on rigid control of the students' classroom behavior, and they try to use rewards and punishments to get students to study. In contrast, teachers with a high sense of self-efficacy create opportunities for success. They know that past successes strengthen the belief that future success is possible, which may encourage students to do what it takes to succeed.

A third line of research has shown that academic self-efficacy beliefs are associated with several other aspects of motivation. These include observation learning from role models, explanatory style, goal setting, and self-esteem. Self-efficacy beliefs also seem to be related to actual improvements in school performance. The beliefs may have this effect by influencing the amount of effort students put into their schoolwork and the degree to which they stick with it, even when problems arise.

Self-efficacy and health

A large body of research has also looked at the

relationship between self-efficacy beliefs and health. In healthy people, a strong sense of self-efficacy can help them adopt a lifestyle that promotes wellness and prevents disease. In people with a chronic illness, self-efficacy beliefs can help them manage pain and other symptoms, reduce the stress associated with being ill, and improve their overall quality of life.

In a 2002 article, Bandura explained the benefits for health promotion and disease prevention: "By managing their health habits, people can live longer, healthier, and slow the process of aging. To stay healthy, people should exercise, refrain from smoking, reduce the amount of dietary fat, keep blood pressure down, and develop effective ways of coping with stressors." Of course, most people know about the benefits of healthy lifestyle habits. Turning that knowledge into action is not always easy, though. High perceived self-efficacy helps people have the confidence to make needed changes and the determination to stick with them.

One interesting line of research has looked at public health messages that are aimed at getting people to make healthy lifestyle changes. There are several possible approaches: giving people factual information, instilling fear, changing people's perception of the risks involved, or enhancing people's perceived self-efficacy. Research has shown that the most effective messages increase people's belief that they have some control over their own health. Scare tactics, on the other hand, do not seem to work as well.

Self-efficacy beliefs also may affect health by influencing how people respond to potentially stressful situations. When someone is faced with a threat—real or imagined, psychological or physical —the threat sets off an alarm in the person's brain, which reacts by preparing the body for defensive action. The pulse quickens, breathing deepens, the senses become sharper, and the muscles tense as the person prepares to fight or flee. In a real emergency, this physiological stress response can be a literal lifesaver. If the response continues over a long period of time, however, it can take a toll on the body, increasing the risk of depression, heart attack, stroke, various aches and pains, and perhaps even cancer. This kind of chronic stress can occur when people have trouble coping with long-term pressures, such as family conflicts, work or school demands, money problems, and the like.

Social-cognitive theory views stress as the result of a perceived inability to have any control over a threatening situation. If people believe they can deal effectively with a situation, it does not lead to stress. It is only when people believe they cannot control an unpleasant situation that they get stressed out by it. Therefore, the higher people's sense of self-efficacy, the less stress they are likely to feel, and fewer stress-related medical problems they are apt to develop.

For people who are already ill, a strong sense of self-efficacy can help them better manage their symptoms and stick to their treatment plan. Studies have shown benefits from perceived self-efficacy in a wide range of medical situations, such as recovering from a heart attack, coping with cancer, taking medication as prescribed, sticking to a rehabilitation program, reducing cholesterol in the diet, controlling arthritis pain, managing diabetes, and eliminating muscle tension headaches.

Such benefits are particularly relevant today, when the burden of chronic disease is heavier than at any other time in history. People are living longer than ever, but this also means that more people are developing age-related chronic illnesses, such as heart disease, osteoarthritis, type 2 diabetes, and cancer. These illnesses are among the most common and costly—but also most preventable—of all medical conditions.

According to the Centers for Disease Control and Prevention, chronic diseases now cause major limitations in activity for more than one out of every 10 Americans. They also account for more than 75% of all medical care costs in the United States. Anything that can reduce this burden is tremendously helpful to individual patients, their families, and society at large. High perceived self-efficacy is one factor that seems to help, both by promoting health and by giving people the confidence they need to cope with a disease.

Collective self-efficacy

Individuals are not the only people who hold beliefs about their own efficacy. Organizations, companies, and even whole nations have beliefs about what they can and cannot achieve when their members work together. These beliefs can profoundly impact current actions and future success of the groups. As Bandura wrote in *Self-Efficacy in Changing Societies*:

> People's beliefs in their collective efficacy influence the type of social future they seek to achieve, how much effort they put into it, and their endurance when collective efforts fail to produce quick results. The stronger they believe in their capabilities to effect social change the more actively they engage in collective efforts to alter national policies and practices.

Bandura argues that many aspects of modern life serve to undermine people's sense of collective self-efficacy. At the national level, a nation's economic and political welfare are often directly affected by events halfway around the world. Unfortunately, it is hard for people to feel they have much control over events that occur so far away. Closer to home, the social structure of modern society can also frustrate people's efforts to act as a group. Government is organized by bureaucracy, and large corporations are complex mazes of subsidiaries, divisions, and departments. It can be daunting to try to bring about change in such complex social settings, and many people simply give up.

However, even in today's world, it is still possible to make a difference through group effort. According to Bandura:

> People who have a sense of collective efficacy will mobilize their efforts and resources to cope with external obstacles to the changes they seek. But those convinced of their collective powerlessness will cease trying even though changes are attainable through perseverant collective action.

THEORIES IN ACTION

Bandura's social-cognitive theory has inspired a vast body of research as well as a large number of practical applications. More than 40 years after Bandura's work on social-cognitive theory, it is still giving rise to lively debates, active research programs, and innovative treatment approaches.

Research

Bandura first became known for the clever design of his Bobo doll experiments. His theorizing has remained firmly grounded in research ever since. Over the years, Bandura has published more than 240 journal articles and book chapters, many of which describe original research. In addition, Bandura's concepts have attracted hundreds of other researchers as well.

As of 2004, an Emory University website devoted to self-efficacy theory listed 83 researchers in the field of educational self-efficacy alone. Even more impressive, it listed 344 graduate students currently conducting self-efficacy research. Their research projects involved self-efficacy beliefs as they related to a wide range of topics, including academics, career, collective action, computers and technology, creativity, gifted education, language arts and literacy, leisure activities, health, mathematics and science, music, motivation, organizations and business, social and psychological issues, special education, spirituality, sports and exercise, and teaching.

The whole scope of this research would be impossible to cover here. However, a few representative studies are described below. These studies provide a small glimpse of the kinds of studies that are currently being done on self-efficacy and social-cognitive theory.

Study of occupational self-efficacy Bandura and his followers claim that self-efficacy beliefs have a big effect on how people actually do their jobs. Some of the strongest evidence for this effect comes from studies in which people's opinions of their own abilities are artificially raised or lowered. For example, in a study published in the *Journal of Personality and Social Psychology* in 1991, Bandura and a colleague presented 60 graduate business students with a computer simulation of a furniture-making business. In the simulation, students were asked to play the role of manager and make decisions based on information about the manufacturing process, weekly orders, and available employees. The goal of the activity was to use goal setting, feedback, and social rewards to motivate the "employees" and maximize production.

The students were told that they would get feedback about how well they were doing at certain points in the activity. Their score was displayed on the computer screen along with another score that was supposedly the average earned by other participants in the study. The students' own scores were based on their actual performance, but the comparison scores were bogus. Compared to the students' scores, the comparison scores were preprogrammed to be either consistently similar, consistently lower, gradually lower, or gradually higher. During the simulation, the students were also asked to respond to computerized surveys about their self-beliefs.

When students were led to believe that they had gradually surpassed the comparison group, they reported an increase in their perceived self-efficacy. They also outperformed the students in the other groups. Within the simulation, they showed improvements in using efficient thinking strategies, setting challenging goals, and having positive emotional self-reactions to their own performance. In contrast, when students were led to believe that they had gradually fallen behind the comparison group, their actual performance suffered. Just changing how these students viewed their abilities seemed to alter their behavior in a way that could spell the difference between business success and failure in the real world.

Study of educational self-efficacy Self-efficacy has also been studied in schools. In one study published in the *Journal of Personality and Social Psychology* in 1999, Bandura and his Italian colleagues looked at 282 children from two middle schools near Rome. The children were asked to fill out several questionnaires that assessed their perceived self-efficacy, depression, and other factors. Teachers and other students also rated the children's behavior and depression, and the children's academic performance was graded by their teachers. One to two years later, the children's depression was assessed again.

The researchers found that children with a low sense of their own academic and social efficacy were more prone to depression than those with a high sense. This was true at the time depression was first assessed, and it was still true one to two years later. In the short run, the children's depression seemed to be related mainly to their perceived lack of academic ability. In the long run, low perceived self-efficacy seemed to keep the depression going by way of poor academic achievement and behavior problems, such as aggressiveness, hyperactivity, anxiety, and withdrawal. A perceived lack of social skills also had an impact on depression, but the effect was stronger in girls than in boys.

On the other hand, children with a strong belief in their own abilities benefited in several ways. They were able to better manage their schoolwork, which led to higher grades. They also had good social skills and few behavior problems. When it comes to school, Bandura says that a strong sense of self-efficacy can motivate students to do their best and help them bounce back from occasional disappointments. It also seems to help protect them from developing depression.

Study of health self-efficacy One way in which self-efficacy beliefs are thought to affect physical health is by helping people take good care of themselves. When people with high perceived self-efficacy do become ill, they are better equipped to cope with their symptoms, which can reduce their stress and suffering in the short term. If the disease lasts for the long term, strong self-management skills can also help people feel better, maintain a more active lifestyle, and stick to their treatment plan. Over time, this kind of self-care may also help halt or slow the worsening of their disease and perhaps ward off serious complications.

For the past two decades, Kate Lorig and her colleagues at the Stanford University School of Medicine have been studying the effects of a patient education program for people with arthritis and other chronic illnesses. Lorig's program is based on self-management education. Rather than simply providing people with facts, it teaches them problem-solving skills. The underlying concept is that teaching people to cope with common disease-related problems enhances their sense of self-efficacy. This, in turn, improves their ability to adapt to the disease effectively.

Research has shown that Lorig's self-management program leads to better medical outcomes than ones that simply provide information. For example, Lorig's program has been shown to improve pain control in people with arthritis, enhance blood glucose control in people with diabetes, and reduce disability in people with a range of medical conditions. Some studies have also found that the program can reduce medical costs.

Empowerment programs Thousands of studies have now shown the many benefits of high perceived self-efficacy in a wide range of situations.

The studies, in turn, have spurred the development of both individual therapies and group programs aimed at helping people get a more accurate sense of their own abilities. In one way or another, many of these approaches center around empowerment. In other words, the goal is to help participants become aware of their power to have some control over the environment and other people as well as to accomplish what they need to do. Of course, these ideas are also at the heart of Bandura's social-cognitive theory, including his concept of self-efficacy.

Employees can be empowered to take responsibility for their personal work. In the same way, students can be empowered to take charge of their own learning, based on guidance from their teachers. And medical patients can be empowered to accept responsibility for managing their own conditions and solving their own problems, based on information from their doctors. One implication of this approach is that people are active players in their own lives.

Programs designed to increase empowerment help people improve their problem-solving and decision-making skills. However, they also help people develop the sense of self-efficacy they need in order to put these skills to good use. Lorig's chronic disease self-management program is an excellent example of a research-based empowerment program. It is also a prime example of Bandura's ideas about human agency and self-efficacy put into practical use.

Modeling therapy Bandura's theories have also been applied to individual therapy. The best-known example is modeling therapy, in which someone with a psychological disorder is given a chance to observe a model cope with the same issues in a healthy way. In particular, this idea has been used for the treatment of phobias, or irrationally intense fears. With modeling therapy, the client is given a chance to watch a model interact with the feared object.

Bandura's early research in this area involved people with an irrationally strong fear of snakes. The client would look through a window into a laboratory room. In that room, there would be a chair and a table, on which sat a latched cage containing a clearly visible snake. The client would then observe the person who was serving as a model slowly approach the snake. The model would act terrified at first, but then appear to pull himself together and start over. Eventually, the model would reach the point where he could open the cage, remove the snake, sit down in the chair, and drape the snake around his neck. All the while, the model would be giving himself calming instructions.

After the client had observed all this, he would be invited to try it himself. The client would be aware that the model was an actor, not a person with a true phobia. Nevertheless, just seeing someone go through the motions of overcoming a phobia was very powerful. Many clients were able to imitate the whole routine after watching the model.

One drawback to this approach is its complexity. It requires not only a therapist, but also an actor, props, and two rooms with a window between them. To simplify the process, Bandura and his students have tested versions of the therapy using recordings of actors. They have also tried having therapists guide clients through the process in their imagination. These methods proved to be almost as effective as using live models.

Research on media violence Bandura's early work on observational learning helped inspire a host of studies on the influence of media violence. This continues to be a timely topic. Studies have shown that even children's television shows contain about 20 violent acts each hour. It comes as no surprise, then, that children who watch a lot of TV tend to think of the world as a scary and dangerous place.

Research has shown that children tend to behave differently after watching violent programs on television. Specifically, children who have watched violent shows are more likely to strike out at playmates, argue, and disobey authority figures than those who have watched nonviolent programs. Children are also less willing to wait patiently for things after viewing TV violence.

In addition, long-term research by Leonard Eron and his colleagues suggests that the effects of television violence may be quite lasting. The researchers found that children who watched hour after hour of TV violence while in elementary school tended to act more aggressively as teenagers. They also were more likely to be arrested and tried for criminal acts as adults.

Findings such as these helped spur the development of the V-chip, technology that lets parents block television programming they do not want their children to see. Most TV shows are now given a rating, which is encoded into the program. The V-chip technology reads this rating and blocks the TV set from showing programs that do not meet whatever rating standards have been selected by the parents. As of January 1, 2000, the Federal Communications Commission required all new television sets 13 inches (33 cm) or larger that are sold in the United States to contain V-chip technology.

CHRONOLOGY

1925: Born on December 4, 1925, in Mundare, Alberta, Canada.

1949: Receives a bachelor's degree from the University of British Columbia.

1952: Receives a PhD in clinical psychology from the University of Iowa. Married Virginia Varns.

1953: Takes a job as a psychology instructor at Stanford University.

1954: Birth of his daughter Mary.

1958: Birth of his daughter Carol.

1959: Publishes his first book, *Adolescent Aggression,* with Richard Walters.

1963: Publishes *Social Learning and Personality Development,* which summarized his research on observational learning and the Bobo doll experiments.

1964: Becomes a full professor at Stanford.

1977: Publishes *Social Learning Theory,* which aroused interest in social learning and modeling.

1974: Serves as president of the American Psychological Association.

1986: Publishes *Social Foundations of Thought and Action: A Social Cognitive Theory,* which described his social-cognitive theory of human functioning.

1997: Publishes *Self-Efficacy: The Exercise of Control,* which set forth his ideas about self-efficacy beliefs.

While the V-chip is helpful, it is far from a complete solution to the problem. Not every parent chooses to use the technology. In addition, violence is also depicted in movies as well as video and computer games. There are still plenty of opportunities for children to learn violent and aggressive behavior by watching role models in the media.

Research on positive media effects If media images are so powerful, why not put them to good use? That is the question asked by other researchers who have tried to use media role models to teach positive behaviors. Using social learning principles, these researchers have developed long-running television and radio series that have aired around the world. The series have been aimed at social goals such as reducing the spread of HIV, slowing population growth, preventing unwanted pregnancies, encouraging literacy, and empowering women.

The programs depict likable characters whose positive actions bring about good results. There are also unsavory villains whose negative actions have the opposite effect. In addition, there are role models who start out behaving badly, but who gradually adopt more positive behavior as the show goes on. The aim is to teach by showing the consequences of positive behavior rather than by lecturing viewers about them. The programs also give viewers information about where to turn for real-world help if they need it.

Research indicates that such "entertainment-education" programs may really make a difference. For example, an organization called Population Communications International airs television and radio programs in countries such as China, India, Kenya, Mexico, and Peru. The organization also conducts controlled studies to track changes in audience behavior. In Mexico and Kenya, dramas revolving around family planning were associated with real-life increases in new users of contraception. In Tanzania, a drama about the spread of HIV was associated with a real-world drop in number of sex partners.

Bandura says that such results should teach psychology a lesson. In a 2002 article in *Monitor on Psychology,* Bandura was quoted as saying, "The problem we have in psychology is that we don't profit from our successes. We construct theories and clarify how they produce their effects, but we lack implementation models for translating theory into effective practice." When people do find creative ways to put theory into practice, however, it is clear that the results are often well worth the effort.

Case studies

Bandura is known mainly as a theorist and researcher. However, he sometimes uses anecdotes to illustrate key points in his theories. For example, to illustrate the difference between learning a behavior by observation and actually imitating it, Bandura recalled a boy who took part in the Bobo doll experiments:

> There was this one child who had watched the modeled aggression on film. In the experimental room, where the children were tested for how much aggression they would show

spontaneously, he displayed very little aggression. When I was walking back to the nursery school with him, he said, 'You know, I saw a cartoon with Rocky, and Rocky sat on the Bobo doll and he punched it in the nose.' He ran off the entire aggressive repertoire. . .What a striking demonstration of the difference between learning and performance!

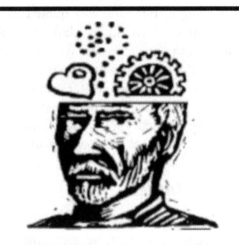

FURTHER ANALYSIS:

Personality theories

Why does one child who watches a violent cartoon hit a playmate afterward, while another plays peacefully? Why does one teenager abuse drugs and alcohol, while another chooses a healthier lifestyle? Why does one employee stay motivated to succeed, while another falls prey to apathy and self-doubt? These are some of the kinds of questions addressed by personality psychology.

Bandura's social-cognitive theory is one example of a personality theory, which attempts to explain what makes people who they are. This type of theory also explores how and why individuals differ from one another. Over the years, a host of different theories have focused on various aspects of personality, including:

- Social dimension—People's ongoing interaction and communication with other individuals around them.

- Cognitive dimension—The way that people think about and actively interpret events in the outside world.

- Ego forces—The conscious part of personality that embodies a person's sense of identity or self.

- Unconscious forces—The part of personality that is not in moment-to-moment awareness, but is still influential.

- Traits, abilities, and skills—The unique set of predispositions and capabilities that a person possesses.

- Conditioning and learning—The way people's behavior is shaped by their experiences and the world.

- Biological dimension—The unique genetic, anatomical, and physiological makeup of an individual.

- Spiritual dimension—People's inward sense of connection to a higher power or meaning that transcends the individual.

Research in this area ranges from laboratory studies of the genetic and biological bases of individual differences to field studies of the social and cultural bases of thoughts, feelings, and behavior. Other studies use the numerous personality tests that have been developed over the decades. And still others are in-depth case studies of individuals or long-term studies that follow a group of people for many years. This is not only a broad area of psychology, but also a deeply fascinating one. It is hard to imagine any subject with more appeal than trying to figure out what it really means to be a person.

Fortunate events and chance encounters In addition, there is one area of interest in which Bandura has relied more heavily than usual on anecdotal evidence: the relationship between personal behavior and fortunate life events. Like so many other people, Bandura has noticed that fortunate events and chance encounters—such as signing up for his first psychology class because it fit his schedule or meeting his wife while golfing—have sometimes changed the whole course of his life.

Bandura also told of one incident in which he was delivering an address about the psychology of chance encounters and life paths. A man entering the lecture hall as it was rapidly filling up grabbed an empty seat. He wound up sitting next to the woman he would later marry—a life-altering chance encounter that took place at a lecture devoted to that very topic.

Bandura has suggested that fortunate events are just one more example of the environmental forces that interact with personal and behavioral factors to shape people's lives. As such, he says the influence of fortunate events could be studied in research like any other kind of environmental variable. He believes that psychology will never be able to predict chance events before they happen. However, psychology can provide a theoretical framework for understanding the impact such events have on people's lives once they have occurred.

FURTHER ANALYSIS:

Self-esteem

Self-esteem is a concept that is closely related to—and sometimes confused with—Bandura's concept of self-efficacy. Nathaniel Branden, a popular theorist in this area, has suggested that a sense of self-efficacy is actually one of two components that make up self-esteem. The other is self-respect, or having a sense of one's value and right to a happy life. Added together, these two components make up self-esteem, which can be defined as the belief that one is both capable of meeting life's challenges and worthy of enjoying happiness.

Few people would dispute that high self-esteem, defined this way, is a good thing. In recent years, however, self-esteem has gotten a bad rap, partly because some people confused it with simply feeling good about oneself. Others confused it with arrogance or conceit, which many psychologists say are actually ways that people with *low* self-esteem try to bolster their shaky confidence.

Several possible methods of enhancing self-esteem have been suggested. For example, affirmations are brief, positive statements that have special meaning for a person, such as "I accept myself as I am" or "I believe in myself." Individuals are often counseled to repeat these statements to themselves several times a day. A second strategy is to associate with positive people who provide encouragement and support. A third strategy is to make a list of past successes, such as passing a difficult test or scoring a goal in a game. This list can then be reviewed periodically as a reminder of the joy and satisfaction the person felt at the time.

Similarly, people can learn to make chance work for them. Bandura notes that people who are openminded, flexible, and venturesome are better able to make the most of unexpected opportunities when they arise. At the same time, those who are able to critically analyze a situation are better equipped to tell a true branch in their life path from a dead end. Therefore, the same kinds of mental abilities that serve people so well at other times can also be quite handy when good fortune comes along.

Relevance to modern readers

Bandura's social-cognitive theory emphasizes that people are capable of self-regulation, or controlling their own behavior. There are three parts to the self-regulation process:

- Self-observation—This involves observing and tracking one's own thoughts, feelings, and behaviors.

- Judgment—This involves comparing oneself to standards. The standards can be set either by oneself or by others.

- Self-response—This involves giving oneself rewards for doing well compared to the standards, or punishments for doing poorly. In general, self-rewards work better than self-punishments.

The three basic principles can be applied to changing almost any undesirable thought or behavior pattern. For example, if a person's problem is an unrealistically low sense of self-efficacy when doing some task, the following steps might help:

- Self-observation—The person should monitor her thoughts, feelings, and behaviors when doing the task in question. For example, if the problem is an unreasonably low sense of self-efficacy for doing math, the person might keep a journal in which she writes down all her negative thoughts, feelings, and physical reactions whenever she is called on in math class, doing math homework, or taking a math test.

- Judgment—The person should make sure her standards for the task are appropriate. If they are too high, she may be setting herself up for failure. If they are too low, on the other hand, she may be shortchanging herself. For example, if the best grade a person has received so far in math class is a C, she might aim for a B on the next test. Aiming for an A+ right off the bat might be too difficult to attain, but aiming for a C+ might be too easy to make much difference.

- Self-response—The person should find ways to celebrate her successes when doing the task, not dwell on her failures. When the person makes a B on the math test, for instance, she should tell herself what a great job she has done. She might also give herself a little treat, such as buying a new CD, going for a bike ride with a friend, or watching her favorite movie again.

For students, a somewhat optimistic view of one's own abilities can make a world of difference.

As Bandura wrote in *Self-Efficacy in Changing Societies*: "The higher the students' beliefs in their efficacy to regulate their own motivation and learning activities, the more assured they are in their efficacy to master academic subjects. Perceived academic efficacy, in turn, promotes intellectual achievement both directly and by raising academic aspirations."

Moreover, Bandura says that students "who have a high sense of efficacy to regulate their own learning and to master academic skills behave more prosocially, are more popular, and experience less rejection by their peers than do [students] who believe they lack these forms of academic efficacy." Clearly, self-efficacy beliefs can have wide-ranging effects. Bandura has been the driving force in explaining what these effects are and how they can be changed through self-regulation.

BIBLIOGRAPHY

Sources

Bandura, Albert. "The Changing Face of Psychology at the Dawning of a Globalization Era." *Canadian Psychology* 42 (2001): 12–24.

Albert Bandura. Emory University. [cited April 11, 2004]. http://www.emory.edu/EDUCATION/mfp/Bandura.

Bandura, Albert. "Exercise of Personal and Collective Efficacy in Changing Societies." In *Self-Efficacy in Changing Societies,* edited by Albert Bandura. New York: Cambridge University Press, 1995.

Bandura, Albert. "Exploration of Fortuitous Determinants of Life Paths." *Psychological Inquiry* 9 (1998): 95–99.

Bandura, Albert. "Growing Primacy of Human Agency in Adaptation and Change in the Electronic Era." *European Psychologist* 7 (2002): 2–16.

Bandura, Albert. "Human Agency: The Rhetoric and the Reality." *American Psychologist* 46 (1991): 157–62.

Bandura, Albert. "Selective Moral Disengagement in the Exercise of Moral Agency." *Journal of Moral Education* 31 (2002): 101–19.

Bandura, Albert. "Self-Efficacy." In *Encyclopedia*

of Human Behavior: Volume 4, edited by V. S. Ramachaudran. New York: Academic Press, 1994.

Bandura, Albert. "Social Cognitive Theory: An Agentic Perspective." *Annual Review of Psychology* 52 (2001): 1–26.

Bandura, Albert, Claudio Barbaranelli, Gian Vittorio Caprara, and Concetta Pastorelli. "Mechanisms of Moral Disengagement in the Exercise of Moral Agency." *Journal of Personality and Social Psychology* 71 (1996): 364–74.

Bandura, Albert, and Forest J. Jourden. "Self-Regulatory Mechanisms Governing the Impact of Social Comparison on Complex Decision Making." *Journal of Personality and Social Psychology* 60 (1991): 941–51.

Bandura, Albert, and Edwin A. Locke. "Negative Self-Efficacy and Goal Effects Revisited." *Journal of Applied Psychology* 88 (2003): 87–99.

Bandura, Albert, Concetta Pastorelli, Claudio Barbaranelli, and Gian Vittorio Caprara. "Self-Efficacy Pathways to Childhood Depression." *Journal of Personality and Social Psychology* 76 (1999): 258–69.

Bandura, Albert, Dorothea Ross, and Sheila A. Ross. "Transmission of Aggression Through Imitation of Aggressive Models." *Journal of Abnormal and Social Psychology* 63 (1961): 575–82.

Bodenheimer, Thomas, Kate Lorig, Halsted Holman, and Kevin Grumbach. "Patient Self-

Management of Chronic Disease in Primary Care." *JAMA* 288 (2002): 2469–475.

Boeree, C. George. *Albert Bandura.* Shippensburg University. 1998 [cited April 28, 2004]. http://www.ship.edu/~cgboeree/bandura.html.

Evans, Richard I. *Albert Bandura: The Man and His Ideas—A Dialogue.* New York: Praeger, 1989.

Haggbloom, Steven J., Renee Warnick, Jason E. Warnick, Vinessa K. Jones, Gary L. Yarbrough, Tenea M. Russell, *et al.* "The 100 Most Eminent Psychologists of the 20th Century." *Review of General Psychology* 6 (2002): 139–52.

Information on Self-Efficacy: A Community of Scholars. Emory University. January 28, 2004 [cited April 11, 2004]. http://www.emory.edu/EDUCATION/mfp/self-efficacy.html.

Pajares, Frank. *Self-Efficacy Beliefs in Academic Contexts: An Outline.* Emory University. 2002 [cited April 8, 2004]. http://www.emory.edu/EDUCATION/mfp/efftalk.ht

Powers, William T. "Commentary on Bandura's 'Human Agency.'" *American Psychologist* 46 (1991): 151–53.

Smith, Deborah. "The Theory Heard 'Round the World." *Monitor on Psychology* 33 (2002): 30.

Vancouver, Jeffrey B., Charles M. Thompson, E. Casey Tischner, and Dan J. Putka. "Two Studies Examining the Negative Effect of Self-Efficacy on Performance." *Journal of Applied Psychology* 87

(2002): 506–16.

Further readings

Acton, G. Scott. *Great Ideas in Personality.* 2004 [cited April 28, 2004]. http://www.personalityresearch.org.

Boeree, C. George. *Personality Theories.* Shippensburg University. 1998 [cited April 28, 2004]. http://www.ship.edu/~cgboeree/perscontents.html.

Branden, Nathaniel. *The Six Pillars of Self-Esteem.* New York: Bantam, 1994.

Brannon, Linda, and Jess Feist. *Health Psychology: An Introduction to Behavior and Health.* 5th ed. Belmont, CA: Wadsworth, 2003.

Friedman, Howard S., and Miriam W. Schustack. *Personality: Classic Theories and Modern Research.* 2nd ed. Boston: Allyn and Bacon, 2002.

Kids and the Media. American Psychological Association. 2004 [cited April 27, 2004]. http://www.apa.org/topics/topic_kidsmedia.html.

Media Violence and Children. Adults and Children Together Against Violence. 2004 [cited April 20, 2004]. http://www.actagainstviolence.com/mediaviolence.

National Association for Self-Esteem. 2004 [cited April 20, 2004]. http://www.self-esteem-nase.org.

Population Communications International. 2003

[cited April 26, 2004]. http://www.population.org.

Revelle, William. *The Personality Project.* Northwestern University. 2004 [cited April 28, 2004]. http://www.personalityproject.org.

Strickland, Bonnie B., ed. *Gale Encyclopedia of Psychology.* 2nd ed. Farmington Hills, MI: Gale Group, 2000.

CPSIA information can be obtained
at www.ICGtesting.com
Printed in the USA
BVHW061745010920
587793BV00003B/217

9 781375 400558